# 30 Minutes
## ... Before Your Job Interview

**June Lines**

KOGAN
PAGE

First published in 1997
Reprinted 1997, 1998, 2000

Kogan Page Limited
120 Pentonville Road
London N1 9JN

© June Lines, 1997

**British Library Cataloguing in Publication Data**

A CIP record for this book is available from the British Library.

ISBN 0 7494 2368 4

Typeset by Saxon Graphics Ltd, Derby
Printed in England by Clays Ltd, St Ives plc

# CONTENTS

# The 30 Minutes Series

*The Kogan Page 30 Minutes Series* has been devised to give your confidence a boost when faced with tackling a new skill or challenge for the first time.

So the next time you're thrown in at the deep end and want to bring your skills up to scratch or pep up your career prospects, turn to the *30 Minutes Series* for help!

*Titles available are:*

30 Minutes Before Your Job Interview
30 Minutes Before a Meeting
30 Minutes Before a Presentation
30 Minutes to Boost Your Communication Skills
30 Minutes to Succeed in Business Writing
30 Minutes to Master the Internet
30 Minutes to Make the Right Decision
30 Minutes to Prepare a Job Application
30 Minutes to Write a Business Plan
30 Minutes to Write a Marketing Plan
30 Minutes to Write a Report
30 Minutes to Write Sales Letters

*Available from all good booksellers.*
*For further information on the series, please contact:*

Kogan Page, 120 Pentonville Road, London N1 9JN
Tel: 0171 278 0433 Fax: 0171 837 6348

# INTRODUCTION

You have been offered an interview. Congratulations! Now you want to ensure that it achieves your objective: the offer of a job.

This book can be read in thirty minutes. It is full of practical tips for turning your interview into an offer of the job you seek. All the suggestions arise from the experience of candidates, employers, recruitment specialists, as well as some interviewers who rarely have to perform and are consequently less practised.

All employers will have their own recruitment methods, and you can never be sure exactly how interviews will be organised. The usual procedures are outlined here and organisations will pick and mix their own selection. For 'organisation' read any employer, of any size, from the local print shop to BT, including schools, hospitals, research establishments, non-profit organisations and local councils.

If you haven't thirty minutes to spare right now, start by checking the list of dos and don'ts below. Good luck!

## **Do**

Be on time
Look neat and well
   groomed
Be well prepared
Look interested and alert
Be yourself

Be honest
Listen carefully
Speak up
Be polite at all times
Smile now and then
Sell yourself

## **Don't**

Be late
Be cluttered
Slouch in your chair
Sniff
Mumble
Lie – but also don't
   volunteer damaging
   information

Undersell yourself
Argue
Ask about travel
   expenses until they
   have been offered
Put on an act

**1**

# LOOK THE PART

A good first impression is the best start you can make. If interviewers find you pleasant to look at, you have already scored points. A well-groomed look pays dividends in those first few minutes.

## Preparation

The night before the interview, check your:

- Clothes (colour, exposure, buttons on, clean and pressed)
- Shoes (cleaned and polished, not in need of repair)
- Hair (does it need washing?)
- Finger nails (clean and trimmed, buffed)
- Jewellery (minimal).

Unless you are sure the organisation would appreciate

power dressing or an obviously new outfit, these are best avoided.

## Safe bets

- White shirt or blouse

- Old school/regimental tie

- Black shoes for men; black court shoes, medium heel, for women

Large people should wear clothes that have a slimming effect, such as long jackets or blouses. Thin people need to enlarge their profile; no employer will be happy with someone who looks as though they have a health problem.

Jeans, overalls, high fashion and smart suits all have their place in interviews for different jobs. Whatever you wear should be neat, clean and not obviously in need of repair. Women need to avoid anything very tight or transparent. If you are down on your luck, borrow or see what a charity shop can offer at low price.

*You* will choose what clothes to wear. Some organisations have an image which is part of company culture. They will possibly not want your very individual style and personality, and seek rather for people who will 'fit'. If you cannot see yourself adapting to their requirements, write them off and start again.

Other employers will appreciate your wacky style, but do not take chances at interviews – tone it down until the job is yours! *Then* experiment when you have summed up the house style. That said, those in

he fashion business will probably wear one of their
own creations.

When being interviewed by hitherto male-orien-
ated organisations or professions, women do better
o wear skirts; trousers may be looked on as a threat
o take over, or dominate.

Use a deodorant, but only the lightest scent or
after-shave, if any. One person's passion is another's
allergy and you don't know what the interviewer's
hang-ups are.

How you walk and talk is part of the picture you
present to the receptionist and interviewer. An air of
confidence, however you are shaking inside, will
beget real confidence. Be someone who is looked at
when they enter – stand up straight, hands out of
pockets, and walk tall. You want to stand out in the
interviewer's memory.

**2**

# WHAT TO TAKE WITH YOU

As part of your keen and eager look, avoid carrying clutter. Just take the essentials – handbag, briefcase, sample case, toolkit, portfolio. Just one – no more. You need a hand free. Prepare it the night before.

Did you keep copies of any documents sent with your application?

- CV (curriculum vitae – your personal history)

- Application form

- Cover letter.

Take these with you, as well as the original advertisement or job description that you have. We tend to slant the different versions of our CV in the direction of the job being applied for, so you really need a copy of the particular one sent, for reference.

## Remember to pack

■ The letter inviting you to come for interview, which confirms the address and telephone number; if there was no letter, take a note of these details; it is dangerous to rely on memory, and you may need to phone them en route.

■ Map, route notes, special instructions

■ Phone card and coins for a call box

■ Notepad and pen to make notes during the interview and record the names of people you met

■ Any company catalogues or brochures, which you will have studied before the interview.

### Evidence of your ability and skill

Suggestions are given in the following list. Show them to the interviewer when you are invited to. If you are questioned about your work, say, 'I have some examples here which you may care to see.' Have them easily accessible, so you don't take up the interviewer's time fumbling with wrappings or knots.

■ Portfolio of drawings, designs, photographs, advertisements you originated, articles you wrote (though some of these may have been submitted with your original application)

■ Specimens of your work, such as word-processed layouts, videos you made, books you edited.

All the above should have your name and address

11

sticker attached, in case you are asked to leave an item for closer inspection.

- Certificates, diplomas
- Press cuttings
- .Testimonials

Do not leave originals of the last three items – ask them to take photocopies while you are there.

On arrival, you may find that you are expected to fill in a separate application form. This is where your copy CV etc comes in useful. The information will need to be neatly transferred to the application form, possibly being reworked to meet the employer's format.

- A list of questions may offer a memory aid at the end of the interview when you are free to ask for further information. See Chapter 6.

If an umbrella is essential on the day of the interview, take a dark-coloured plastic bag with you too, to thrust the wet umbrella into on arrival, and avoid the need to leave it around, and possibly forget it on your way out. The bag can be left on the same hanger as your coat.

**3**

# GET THERE ON TIME

For students, the first interview may take place at their own campus. This chapter is addressed to interviewees who have appointments in unfamiliar surroundings.

You will have confirmed in writing – time permitting – the date and time of the appointment, so they know to expect you.

Apart from not turning up at all – and not phoning to explain or apologise – the worst thing you can do is to be late. It makes a poor impression on the interviewer and starts you off at a disadvantage, as well as upsetting their timetable.

### The night before

- Prepare your clothes
- Get your briefcase or bag ready
- No partying

- Arrange two wake-up calls in case one fails
- Have a good night's sleep.

## Try to do a dummy run

Always aim to be at least ten minutes early; anything more looks like anxiety. We all know that trains can be delayed, traffic gridlocked, but many difficulties can be avoided by a previous test run if time allows. Phone and ask the interviewer the nearest station, bus stop or parking space if this information has not been provided.

### Going on foot

Walk the route beforehand, time yourself, and be sure you find the right entrance to the building.

### Using the bus

Try the journey in advance, checking actual times against the timetable, and making sure you know the right stop to alight. You don't want to end up running a mile because you got off too late or too soon.

### Train or Underground

Check the timetables and allow for cancellation or delay. A main line train ticket can be bought the day before to avoid ticket office queues, but London Underground tickets are valid only on the day of purchase, so be prepared to wait.

Ceefax page 432 can be checked for hold-ups on

the railways; page 436 offers the same service for London Underground.

## Car travel

Make sure you:

- Know the route
- Have the route written down if a long journey is involved
- Have enough petrol
- Listen to local radio to be forewarned of any problems on the way.

## Long-distance travel

Where an overnight stay is involved and you do not know the area, a good briefing from the interviewer is essential. Some will send a map.

## Meeting the receptionist

Receptionists are often asked what impressions they have gained of visitors. A friendly greeting will help to fix you in their memory; so will grumpiness, a strong smell of garlic, tobacco or alcohol. Avoid them all.

You may have to sign in and get a security pass.

'Good morning. My name is Margaret Whitworth and I have an appointment with George Williams at 11.15. I'm a bit early; perhaps I could tidy myself before seeing him.'

An appearance check in the washroom will ensure

you look your best. See you have no splashes if the day is wet. Take a few deep breaths and relax.

Chat to the receptionist only if she or he is not busy and seems forthcoming.

It is dangerous to make more than one appointment in the same morning or afternoon because:

■ The interview timetable may be running late (in which case you will probably be offered refreshments)

■ Successful interviewees may be asked to have a second meeting or test straight away.

Use any spare waiting time to prepare yourself:

■ Review your application or CV

■ Study wall displays or showcases which will tell you more about the organisation

■ Read any company literature put out for visitors

■ Study the people passing through

■ Listen to the receptionist; does the organisation sound the sort of place you would like to work in?

■ Breathe deeply to stay calm.

If the receptionist does not relieve you of your coat, take it with you to the interview.

You are now ready to present yourself to the interviewer.

# 4

# MEETING THE INTERVIEWER OR PANEL

The interview is designed to find out whether you are the best person to do the job. It is usually held on a one-to-one basis, but be prepared to meet a panel.

You will approach the interview with greater confidence if you have been able to practise beforehand. Even better, back up this practice with information you have discovered about what the job involves and the employer.

Do you know anyone connected with your target organisation? Working there, supplying goods and services, subcontracting, with a son or daughter there? See if you can pick their brains for more information. Anyone with inside knowledge could help you to shine at interview.

The public library reference section will be useful for research. Annual directories give names of senior personnel; products of manufacturing and mining companies will be listed, as well as their worldwide activities. Local newspapers may be stored or held on film, and a look at the index will tell you if the organisation has been in the news. Extel, or a public limited company's annual report (which you send for), shows its financial situation and reveals the spread of its interests and profitability.

## A practice interview

Try doing a mock interview with a friend, and practise over and over again those areas in which they said you were weakest.

If the job stakes are high, you may consider it worth having a session with a professional consultant who will offer image advice and rehearse an interview with you.

## Communication skills

The ability to communicate is important for most jobs. You will score points if you can:

- Appear at ease with other people

- Initiate conversation

- Answer with confidence

- Express yourself well.

All these skills contribute to the overall impression you give.

## Greeting

You will probably be collected from reception by the interviewer or an assistant, who may shake hands. Always respond with a firm but not punishing grip.

'Anthony Moore? How do you do. I am Jocelyn Mason, Mr Graham's assistant, and will take you to him.'

Smile. Respond. 'How do you do.'

Remember these names. They could be useful to drop into a later conversation, if it comes naturally, and when or if you write and thank the interviewer afterwards.

If you are asked to find your own way to the interview room, 'Please go to the second door on the left along the corridor', knock firmly if the door is shut, and then enter.

'Anthony Moore? Glad to meet you. I'm George Graham; we spoke on the telephone.'

Sit down when invited, not before. If the light in your eyes is too strong, shift the chair slightly to be more comfortable. Don't be intimidated by an interrogation set-up, but move slightly.

If two people are in the room, but only one addresses you throughout the interview, try to make eye contact with both.

## Body language

It is important to look alert and interested all the time. Lean slightly forward in your chair. Use your hands naturally, not to clutch yourself with – this looks as though you are holding back.

Look interested even if the job sounds boring or not at all what you want. Find out more when it is your turn to ask questions.

## Who will interview?

This interview may be the only one, or the first of two or more. Depending on the set-up, any one of the following might carry it out:

- Your future employer/boss
- A personnel manager
- A departmental manager
- A panel of two or more (up to eight)
- The person you are replacing (who is being promoted)
- A recruitment consultant
- An occupational therapist.

There may be two interviews on the same day, the first with personnel department, the second with a departmental manager if the first interview goes well. The departmental manager is likely to decide the order of preference, and the job offer will be made to number one, the others being put on hold until an acceptance is received. If number one pulls out or fails a critical test, the offer is made to number two.

Sometimes the initial interview will be carried out by a professional recruitment agency for the employer. This vetting session will be more objective, and the scrutiny of your CV and application form more rigorous. They will ask the questions, passing your name on only if the answers are entirely satisfactory. The employer will then interview the short-list, and the questions *you* want to ask will have to be deferred until this second interview, as the agency will either not know the answers or not be authorised to go into detail.

As agencies act for a variety of employers, they are likely to note your details if you impressed them in case a suitably senior post is on offer in the future.

High street employment agencies are not in this league, and their candidates will be interviewed in depth by the employer.

## The interview

A few general remarks to make you feel at home may be accompanied by an offer of coffee. Accept it if you have enough command over your nerves to drink it without spilling or rattling the cup in the saucer. A refusal can look like lack of confidence. You choose! However, do not smoke, chew gum or eat goodies from your pocket. The warning may sound superfluous, but they have all been witnessed by amazed interviewers.

The small talk will be along the lines of:

'What was your journey like?'

'How did you get here from the station?'

'Not good weather for travelling today. Were there any hold-ups?'

Long replies are not called for; smile and speak

clearly. Put the cup and saucer down carefully when you have finished.

The interviewer should tell you about the organisation, the job, and describe basic terms and conditions, as well as promotion possibilities. You may be given a tour of the building.

In some circumstances, applicants may be better at interviews than the employer, either through their greater experience or the employer's lack of it. Such an interview is likely to be unstructured, and you may be able to guide the course of it instead of simply sitting down to a friendly chat during which you learn little. If you have natural confidence, be careful not to let it appear as arrogance or self-satisfaction, which may be seen as a threat to someone already in post. People don't like to feel dominated by newcomers.

## Panel interviews

These may take you aback if you are not expecting to be faced by more than two people. They are most often used in education, medicine, the armed services and public service sectors, and increasingly in business, even when the job being filled is not a high level one. Don't be daunted.

One will lead the questioning, but all will have been circulated with your details and may question you in turn. A more thorough investigation of your CV or application form results.

Sit up straight and look them in the eye when they address you, but try not to speak back only to the person who asked the question. Let your glance sweep along.

Panel members are often not trained interviewers although some will have a battery of questions to be covered during your time with them. Candidates may suffer from the really inadequate ones. One chairman started off by asking, 'What salary are you expecting?' The candidate felt that the job should have been described first, and the salary range included in the advertisement or discussed when an offer was being made, before this question was asked. You need to be prepared to handle this.

They will question you on your CV and ask for elucidation of certain matters, sometimes with a view to checking for truth, honesty or exaggeration. One member may have been to your school or college, graduated at your university, known your previous managing director or someone else where you have worked. If the interview goes well, they will probably follow this lead up with a phone call later to get an 'insider' view of you. This is especially true in certain professions and businesses.

Occasionally, a panel will seem totally uninterested in your CV, and you will wonder if they have even read it. It is just possible that they have decided already who should be offered the job, but the rules insist that the vacancy is published and a number of interviews must take place, so when you appear they are just marking time. You will never prove it, just have suspicions. Put this hard luck down to experience.

## Discrimination and preference

The law aims to prevent discrimination on the

grounds of race, gender, disability and, in some circumstances, religion. Professional recruiters will be aware of the implications if equal consideration is not given to all candidates presenting equally proven skills, qualifications and experience.

The questions interviewers ask must not be slanted to the disadvantage of any group, but if you are a mother returning to work after bringing up a family, you will probably realise that the interviewer needs reassurance that you have good arrangements in place to cover for school holidays and emergencies, and provide it without being asked, even though your husband would not be asked the same question.

Equal opportunity employers tend to place more emphasis on attitude, and award more points for indications that a good team member is facing them; checking on skills and experience can be a lower priority, as they feel they can train up people with the right attitude to the job.

## Who will be chosen?

The successful candidate is not necessarily the most highly skilled, best qualified, or a member of Mensa. The winner may be the one who comes across as reliable, motivated, proficient, able to work well with others, and get the best results from colleagues and subordinates.

The next chapter discusses the questions most often put to candidates. Remember that employers look for profits and cost savings, so relate your answers to these needs.

# 5

# DEALING WITH CORE QUESTIONS

Employers are looking for someone to do the job well, not for problem people. Your role is to persuade them that you are the answer to *their* problem, so it is important to:

- Look enthusiastic
- Emphasise your strengths and achievements
- Play down your weaknesses
- Smile now and then.

Always listen carefully to the questions to avoid misunderstandings.

The easy ones come first, even though the answers may already be on file:

- How did you hear about the job?

- Why do you want it?

- Do you know anyone in the company?

Good interviewers use a mix of open and closed questions. Open questions give the candidate scope to expand the information offered:

- What was your school like?

- How did you get your present job?

Closed questions require a short answer, one word even, or a date:

- How old are you now?

- Do you have a clean driving licence?

Concise answers are required, even for open questions; the interviewer hasn't time to listen while someone rambles on, giving a poor impression of their communication skills. Practise your answers to all the questions in this book, so you are prepared.

## Age

If you are young, interviewers will be encouraged by an air of stability: neat dress, a willingness to learn, a serious attitude to the job and respect for authority.

If your age is against you – you are adrift in the job market at fifty – do realise that you may be working under people considerably younger than yourself, and for less money than you were used to getting. The employer will need to be reassured that you will be flexible and accept the situation gracefully, especially if:

- you need to acquire new skills on the job

- your knowledge and experience exceed those of your new superior.

Appearance will count for a great deal, and a trim figure is an advantage. Someone with patience and maturity can be a source of strength in a 'young' department, and provided you are not regarded as intimidating, you may be welcomed for that reason.

## The questions

Depending on your position in the job market, different questions will be put to you, and you could be asked to take tests. These are discussed in Chapter 10.

This chapter offers a selection of questions for the following job seekers:

- First jobbers

- Job changers and career movers

- Returners to work

- Unemployed job hunters.

Unusual or unexpected achievements remain in the interviewer's memory and may tip the score if the shortlisted candidates are all equally good, but unremarkable. Can you drop one into your responses?

Questions about your interests are designed to find out the *sort* of person you are:

- Active or passive (player or observer)

- Active in solo or team activities
- An outdoor type
- Mechanically minded
- Intellectual.

Interviewers will be taking notes or marking you – don't be put off by this, you can make notes too – evaluating you on all or any of the following:

- Appearance
- Ability to express yourself
- Achievements and experience
- Education and training
- Work history
- Performance in present job
- Aptitudes
- Personality
- Family background and upbringing.

### First jobbers

Most interviewers will allow for inexperience and nervousness, but even they cannot gain a good impression if you are very shy or tongue-tied. If you know this is your problem, ask a family member or friend to do a practice session with you beforehand, to give yourself a better start. Practise relaxation too.

School and college leavers may have had a paper round, Saturday job or worked in the holidays, so make sure this useful experience is known to the interviewer. It shows that you are used to the discipline of work – being on time, working for several hours at a stretch.

Try to find out in advance what this particular job involves, either by talking to someone doing it – or something similar – or by reading up leaflets and books in your careers library.

## Questions

- Tell me about your school/college.

- Did you have a good attendance record?

- Were you offered the chance to take GCSEs?

- Which subjects do you feel you could have passed, given the opportunity?

- Did you do as well in A levels as you expected?

- Why did you decide to do business studies for BTEC?

- What special projects did you undertake at school?

- Did you consider applying for Youth Training?

- What do you really want to do in life?

- Do you see your hobbies/interests/sport as separate from work or connected with it?

- What was involved in your Saturday job with Safeway?

- Do you live with your parents?

- Do you have any brothers or sisters?

- Are they older or younger than you?

- Do your parents work? What do they do?

- Are you ambitious?

- Do you plan to continue your education later on?

- Have you considered a vocational course?

A school reference will probably be asked for, in the absence of work experience. Give the name of your head.

If you were in care or had a disrupted childhood, and this motivates you to do well at work and build a new life for yourself, can you put this across to the interviewer? If so, allowances will probably be made for your less advantageous start in life. Many jobs will offer training for school leavers, especially in organisations which have gained an Investors in People assessment.

## Graduates

Employers who receive large numbers of speculative applications, often on a careers service Standard Application Form, will arrange interviews at universities. Otherwise, you are interviewed in the same surroundings as any other candidate.

Your qualification indicates that you have a well-trained mind. Employers want to know that you will use it to their advantage – that there is a fit between classics and banking, for example. Because they are looking for management trainees they will be assessing management potential, and seek evidence of:

- Ambition
- Leadership
- Good character
- Good judgement
- A sense of responsibility
- Ability to meet challenges
- Decisiveness.

Bring out these qualities in yourself when dealing with questions. You may be asked for examples from your own life when you displayed these characteristics. Have your stories ready! Try to relate them to the job.

### Questions

- Why did you choose your degree subject?
- Why did you prefer Reading when you had an offer from Cambridge?
- What aspects of your course are most relevant to this job?
- What experience did you gain from your vacation work/sandwich course?
- Were you prominent in any university activity or society? Which?

> — Some employers see politically committed candidates as potential troublemakers. Too much interest in sport may be interpreted as a lack of dedication to the job, but on the positive side, builds leadership and teamwork skills. Always emphasise the positive aspects.

- Which of your existing skills do you think will be useful if you come to work for us?

- Why have you applied to this company?
  > — Here is your chance to praise the company and demonstrate what you have learned about it: it seems to be the best, the leader, most reputable, expanding, a good employer, offer outstanding research facilities, etc.

- What do you know about this industry/profession?

- What do you want to be doing in five years' time?
  > — You should have achieved appropriate professional qualifications, deserving of promotion, as well as considerable experience. You look for advancement in your chosen career.

- Tell me about yourself.
  > — Have a short presentation already prepared which you can memorise, so it comes across as spontaneous. Emphasise your sound education, skills, and how they integrate with your leisure activities and career aspirations.

- What are your strengths?

- What are your weaknesses?

— Turn past weaknesses into present strengths. 'I used to...but I realised that...and so I....

■ Describe a tricky situation where, with hindsight, you should have acted differently.

— Have a story ready. If you admit to a mistake, follow this by showing how you remedied it, and present the incident as a learning opportunity from which you have benefited.

■ Describe a difficult situation which you consider you handled well.
— Have an answer prepared.

■ What are your greatest achievements?
— A gift of a question. Make good use of it.

## Job changers and career movers

Job changers may only be looking for their second or third job. Career movers have come to prove themselves worthy of a more senior one. Either way, be prepared for your CV, job history, abilities and qualifications to be picked over in some detail, relative to the level of the job sought.

Teacher interview panels will consist of the head, a governor, possibly the head of department, who will probably have observed the candidates taking a lesson in their present job. For this reason, and the fact that teachers are required to give references, it becomes known to the present employer when a teacher is looking elsewhere.

Remember that every organisation has its own procedures and what you are used to is not necessarily the employer's preference, so avoid dispute on this or any other subject that arises. Two golden rules apply:

1. Never argue with the interviewer.

2. Never openly criticise past employers.

To do so throws doubt on your ability to get on with other people and to handle difficult situations.

The first interview may be the only one for applicants still gaining basic skills and experience. Career movers may find the probing, technical questions saved for a later session.

## Questions

- Why do you wish to leave your present job?

- What exactly do you do?

- What have you achieved in this job?

- Have you learned from this job? What?

- Why have you stayed so long in each job?

- Why have you changed jobs so often?

- What was your attendance record in your last job?

- Did you get promoted in your last job?

- Why did you leave your last job?

- Are you computer literate?

- Do you write your own letters/reports/agreements/press releases?

- Can you handle figures? Prepare budgets? Work out commission?

- What training have you had since starting work?

- Did you ever disagree with your manager?

- How did you resolve the disagreement?

- What was the worst situation you faced?

- How did you deal with it?

- What has been your greatest achievement at work so far?

- What do you dislike doing most at work?

In your responses, always emphasise the positive and avoid criticism of previous employers or complaints about the conditions, so you do not come across as a perpetual moaner. Sound as though you enjoy your work.

Be prepared for the interviewer to pick up an item from the desk: 'Sell me this pen', 'Sell me this paper-clip.' Resist the temptation to snarl, 'I haven't come here to sell pens', do as you are asked, and sell your-self too, as quick witted. Indicate features and bene-fits, give a price. 'How many would you like?', 'Do you want them gift wrapped?'

## Career movers

You are likely to be questioned or tested (or both) more rigorously than other applicants, by higher level people, especially those who will have to work with you. You will be expected to have a record of:

- Ambition
- Decisiveness
- Good problem solving
- Ability to manage yourself and other people
- Understanding of budgets
- Understanding of financial objectives
- Appreciation of the organisation's purpose and how it is to be achieved
- Achievement.

## Questions

- Why are you planning to leave your organisation? Is there no scope for promotion?
- What has been your experience of managing staff?
- How do you react to working under pressure?
- Are you able to undertake travel abroad at short notice?
- What size budgets are you used to handling?
- What control did you have over your department's expenditure?
- Did you engage your own staff?
- What motivates you?
  — They want to know how important status, power, money and achievements are to you.
- Are you good at motivating others?
- What have you achieved in your present job?

Questions will also check your knowledge of the business, profession, trade, etc, experience and/or qualifications, current problems facing your industry, the effects of legislation on it, though many questions along these lines may be held over until a second interview.

## Unemployed job hunters and returners to the workforce

Lack of confidence and self-esteem will probably be your main problem, leading you to underrate your genuine, positive qualities.

### Job hunters

If your unemployment period has been short, your skills will not have suffered, and you will show up as keen to resume work. There will be questions about the reasons for your unemployment, and these need to be handled carefully.

*Redundancy*

Reorganisation, cutbacks, relocation and shutdown are straightforward, provable causes, and questions should not present problems unless very few employees suffered redundancy, in which case the questioner will want to know why you were among those selected.

*Illness, addiction and accident*

Tricky. The new employer will want to know whether you have fully recovered, to be reassured that your work will be done properly. If medical insurance is part of the remuneration package, recent medical history will have to be revealed, and insurers reserve the right to check this out.

A disabled applicant has the right not to be discriminated against purely on the grounds of disability.

*Dismissal*

This is more difficult to handle. Answer questions but don't volunteer too much information. If you are taken on and it is later found that you lied at interview, this is a legitimate cause for dismissal. Try not to appear as someone who can't get on with other people. Consider these:

— It was difficult to get the manager to agree priorities.

— There were differences of opinion about how certain jobs should be done.

— Sales people were always promising more than we could deliver on time, and we took the blame.

Legitimate reasons for dismissal include gross misconduct, so employers will look into this area very severely. Under this heading come fighting, damaging company property, wilful disregard of safety regulations, breaking company rules on alcohol or drugs.

If you took your dismissal case to an industrial tribunal and won it, still be careful how – and if – you tell a new employer about it. Innocent or guilty, you may be labelled 'Troublemaker'.

Some employees effectively dismiss themselves by refusing to carry out reasonable instructions or accepting a ruling (fair or unfair). If this is your experience, what did you learn from it? Practise dealing with these points before your job interview.

Did you just walk out because you couldn't handle a situation? Be prepared to answer this one.

## Questions

- What have you done to find a job?

- Have you taken any course while unemployed, either vocational or in leisure subjects?

- Did you do any voluntary work?

- How have you used the time?

- Do you realise that the vacancy is for a lower level job than you have been used to? How will you adapt?

Take along your file of applications to show you have tried to find a new job and are not work-shy.

*Gaps in your work history*

Were you a carer, convict or long-term patient?

Carers should be quite open about their circumstances, but whatever your gender, see the notes for women returners below.

An employer's attitude to prison sentences will depend largely on the reason for them. If it was totally unconnected with the work you will be doing, the sentence will be noted but may not affect the outcome of the interview. If you undertook training courses in prison, these will show you were motivated enough to take a positive view of your future.

The legal position regarding spent sentences which do not have to be revealed is complicated, and it would be best to obtain advice before making a job application or attending an interview. Some application forms ask specifically about convictions. Remember that lying at interview is a legitimate reason for dismissal, if it is discovered.

## Women returners and carers

Women returners tend not to give themselves credit for the management skills and maturity gained while they have been rearing children or caring for others.

The daily management of a home helps to develop skills directly transferable to a work environment:

- Advance planning

- Scheduling

- Budgeting

- Organising

- Training

- Assessing

- Problem solving

- Soothing ruffled feelings

- Punishing

- Rewarding.

Remind the interviewer that you offer maturity and experience of life.

*Appearance*

Depending on the job you seek, your appearance may need an overhaul. It is so easy to let things drift while you are at home. Try to study the women in places where you aspire to work, and see how you measure up. Do you need a new haircut, a smarter outfit, a less capacious handbag, some neater shoes? Don't shop on the way to the interview – a carrier bag will make it look as if you are still tied to home.

*Skills*

Women who have not worked for some years will find that the technological revolution has changed most people's work, from warehousing and supermarket checkouts to travel agencies, graphic design, financial services and all office work. Some employers provide training, but secretaries will probably be expected to cope with word processing. Can you manage a local authority course if your job skills need honing?

*Interviews*

Rehearse the interview with a friend or family member. If you still feel diffident, try to take a course on assertiveness (not the same as aggression) or read up on controlling anxiety.

If you are offered an interview, accept it, even if the job doesn't sound what you want. You will gain interview experience and may find out where your skills need a boost or how you react to other people already working there.

Before the interview, ensure that arrangements are in place for the continuation of the care you have been offering, if the situation still exists. The employer will want to know what happens to the children when they are sick, on holiday or in trouble. Except in an emergency, they will not expect you to drop everything and rush off, or not report for work. Reassure the interviewer that your excellent organising ability has equipped you to make alternative plans, before the subject arises. You will have proclaimed yourself as a returner, so a gentle question on the matter should not be regarded as discriminatory.

Your work references will be out of date, so do not forget to mention any activities you have undertaken which show you up as capable, such as voluntary work in a parent–teacher association, charity, play group or church group. If you earned money at home, such as selling from a catalogue, that will demonstrate your business sense.

If you are asked why you will do the job well, it's a wonderful chance to match your home experience to the demands of the job, and show you have what it takes.

The best book on interview questions is *Great Answers to Tough Interview Questions* by Martin John Yate (Kogan Page). It will be in your public library.

## 6

# ASKING QUESTIONS

Having told you about the job, outlined the terms and conditions, the interviewer will ask if you have any questions.

You may have no questions at all, so instead of a bald 'No' which may sound like lack of interest, say that the information already provided covers everything you can think of at present.

If you can manage a question or two, it looks better, and shows you have been taking notice.

Select questions with care. If yours all centre on salary, perks and holidays, it looks as though they are all you care about. The employer wants someone dedicated to the job in the first instance, not to the benefits. These questions can be raised once you have an offer if the interviewer has not dealt with them.

### Questions

■ Why is there a vacancy?

- How long was the last person in the job?

- Do you promote internally if suitable candidates exist?

- Are vacancies notified to existing staff?

- Does the company expect to expand in this country or abroad?

If a whole new employment area is being opened up, you can ask about training, but training questions are best avoided if you have presented yourself as skilled and experienced in the particular field. Anyone recruited as a trainee will have a programme prepared for them. If relocation is on the cards, you could raise the issue:

- There are rumours of relocation following the takeover. Have they any foundation?

- Will the company have a relocation package to assist with the move?
  — This should come up when a job offer is made.

Entrants to the professions will want to know if study leave is available before exams, whether days off are allowed for taking the exams, or they are deducted from holidays. For example, actuarial students in insurance companies are likely to be given time, as are accountancy students in the financial services sector, but accountancy students in the manufacturing trades would need to have the situation clarified.

- What opportunities are there to study for further qualifications?

— Day release or block release may be a possibility.

■ What opportunities are there to work in overseas branches?

Questions everyone should feel free to ask:

■ When can I expect to hear from you again?

■ How soon do you expect to make a decision?

■ When would I be expected to start, in the event of an offer?

■ I have two weeks' holiday arranged in September. Would this be any problem?

■ Is there a probationary period before a job is firm?

■ Would any offer be subject to satisfactory references? To any other condition?

Unless you have another point to make, the interview will end here. You may want to mention a prominent person who would speak for you. This is fine provided you don't wave the name like a threat over the personnel manager and don't pretend to a greater acquaintance than you actually have.

Gather up any belongings without fuss, and make a good exit. 'Thank you so much for seeing me' and shake hands if one is offered. 'I look forward to hearing from you.'

Retrieve your coat from reception if it was left there, and thank the receptionist. 'Goodbye.'

# 7

# WE'LL LET YOU KNOW

Were you offered the job straight away?
Congratulations.

Do you want to talk it over with your family or
partner before accepting it, or has the interview left
you with doubts about its suitability for you? Say you
would like to get back to them the following day.

If you are keen to get back to work after a gap in
your CV, and it's not necessarily the job you would
have chosen first, consider that it is easier to get your
next job with some up-to-date experience behind
you. You may find the job offers more than you
expected, as well as a great social life.

See Chapter 11 regarding terms and conditions
which you need to be sure about.

Teachers are lucky in that they usually know the
result on the same day. They may be asked to wait –
all candidates together in one room – or to leave a
contact number for the evening.

## Awaiting a decision

Large organisations often take their time to decide – so long, sometimes, that you will have accepted another offer in the mean time. If number one on their shortlist has accepted another position or had second thoughts, they proceed to number two, and so on. All this time the hot prospects are kept waiting.

To reinforce an interviewer's impression of you, write a note of thanks afterwards – if it went well and you are keen – and say what a pleasure it was to meet and how you look forward to hearing from them. Such a letter is also your chance to offer supplementary information which you overlooked or forgot at the time.

If an organisation is so bureaucratic that it calls candidates for comparatively junior positions to come for several interviews (up to four for a medium-grade secretary in one large American-owned company in Britain) you may reconsider whether it is the place for you. How long will internal decisions take when you are finally in post? Of course, very enticing rewards might be offered and swing your decision in their favour.

Senior positions are subject to many filtering processes, and often several panel interviews, as well as rigorous checking of credentials. A large oil company has been known to require sixteen separate interviews for a high-level, international, bilingual post. There was worldwide competition for this highly remunerated position.

Tests are set by many organisations which short-listed candidates must pass. They can vary from straight skill tests of proficiency with a word processor or mechanical equipment, possibly taken on the same day as the interview, through aptitude and assessments tests, lasting from an hour to two days.

Specially designed tests are set for entrants to the Civil Service, police forces, fire services and the armed forces. More on the subject in Chapter 10.

A professional recruiter or selection agency will prepare a shortlist for the employer, who will ask those on the list to attend a second interview. If the agent does not put your name forward, this is not the end of the line. There may be other possibilities for which your name will be borne in mind.

## Prepare for the next interview

By analysing your first interview, and deciding where you could have done better, you can use the knowledge to polish your performance. Everyone else on the shortlist will be that bit more determined too, so don't underestimate the competition.

Would more knowledge of the organisation have helped you? Research *now* to be ready for next time. Check what you remember and check yourself against this list:

- Did I introduce myself well?

- Did I appear interested and confident?

- Was I happy with my appearance?

- Was I punctual?

- Did I greet the receptionist properly?

- Did I deal with the questions without floundering?

- Did I ramble on too much?

- Was I too serious/too jokey?

- Did I forget anything important?

- Did I thank the interviewer and ask when I would hear?

- Have I remembered the interviewers' names accurately?

Make a note of the questions you remember, and check how much of your CV was covered. What else might be asked next time in relation to the job description?

If you are called for a second interview, check with your referees that you can give their names in the event of a job offer. If you have been warned that you will be expected to take a test next time, prepare yourself by reading Chapter 10.

# 8

# THE SECOND INTERVIEW

Preparation for the second interview is similar to that for the first, as outlined in the early chapters, unless the two happen on the same day. Check through the suggestions for:

- Appearance

- Documents to take with you

- Evidence of ability and skill.

If you can wear a different suit, shirt or blouse, it will indicate that you possess more than one set of respectable clothes. Still stay clutter free.

You may meet the first interviewer again, and your greeting can include a friendly remark, 'How nice to see you again', and use their name.

You will meet one or more senior persons this

time: your manager, the department manager, the managing director for example. They will look to confirm the first interviewer's good opinion of you, and this could be done by a fairly informal chat, checking your personality, background, contacts and knowledge of the business.

More formally, the second interview may take the form of separate tests or further questions, based on technical problems, your opinion of a project asked – real or hypothetical.

You may be asked to work on a project in your own time, especially when translation or creative activities are involved. The candidates' results decide who gets the job offer or moves up into round three.

## Hospitality

Depending on the job, and how well you are regarded, this second meeting could include hospitality – a few drinks, coffee, lunch or dinner. Be yourself, but never be off your guard.

Over a meal with future colleagues, your demeanour, conversational style and social graces will be under observation, especially if the job involves entertaining clients.

Drink alcohol in moderation, even if the others don't. If you are teetotal, ask for a non-alcoholic drink, but avoid giving the impression that you were an alcoholic who is now on the wagon. It could destroy your job chances in an instant. Employers are very wary of alcohol or drug abusers, even if it all happened in the past.

Your ability to keep your head and field difficult questions will be noted. A selection of straightforward questions is given below, but those from earlier sections of the book are also a possibility. Have your answers ready, especially if you were selected by a recruitment agency, and this is your first meeting with the employer.

## Questions

- How do you get on with colleagues?

- Did you recruit your own staff, or was this handled by personnel?

- Have you ever trained your own staff?

- Did you draw up the work rosters for your division?

- What improvements have you made in your present job?

- What cost savings did you achieve in the department?

- How did you increase productivity?

- How did sales improve under your management?

- What was your most successful campaign?

- What was your most disastrous campaign?

- What effect will your working abroad be likely to have on your family? Have you discussed the possibility with them?

- What difference did it make to you when the company became a plc?

- What was your contribution to research on the Numbus project?

If no offer has been made, you can reasonably ask when a decision is likely.

Take your leave of the people you met and make a good exit.

**9**

# TELEPHONE INTERVIEWS

Some job advertisements invite a telephone response, especially if the job involves great use of the phone. It is a way of checking your telephone manner, and a satisfactory conversation may be followed by a request to come for interview or to complete a formal written application.

Before you pick up the phone to dial an advertiser, have your CV by you, so you can answer relevant questions accurately. If you are job hunting, keep the following items near the phone or on you:

- CV

- Letter of application for any job, plus enclosure

- Note pad and pencil

- Diary, so you are prepared to make an appointment.

If you have been sending out different versions of your CV to match different advertisements, it is essential to know which one is being referred to at the time. Don't have your computer skills CV in front of you when the caller is responding to a telesales CV.

Warn others in the house that you are sending out applications, so they can be prepared to take calls in your absence; ask them to fetch you to the phone immediately or take a clear message if you are out – name, number, company name, best time to call back.

Interviewers also use the telephone to vet applicants, whether they have written in on spec or in answer to an advertisement. It is cheaper than face-to-face interviewing, and is a quicker way of making up a shortlist. They may ask for clarification of a point in your CV or application, or simply be using this as the reason for calling to vet your speech and communication skills.

Try not to be flustered when a call comes, and answer the questions. If you can sit comfortably while talking and smile – even though no one can see you – a friendlier image of you will be received at the other end.

Make a note of:

■ The name of the person calling

■ The organisation

■ Address and phone number

■ Directions on how to get there.

If there is time, confirm the arrangement in writing; it looks very efficient.

---

Your address
Phone number
Date

Name of caller
Company address

Dear Mr/Mrs/Ms X

Thank you for telephoning me today regarding the vacancy for a customer service executive, and as arranged, I look forward to meeting you at 10.30 am on Tuesday 20 May at your address.

Yours sincerely

(Your signature)

Your name in clear writing.

---

This is just an example you can adapt to your situation.

If you have to phone back, be prepared for large organisations to answer with recorded messages and a 'menu' which you can access with a press-button phone only. If you still have a dial phone, keep your cool and hold on until the end of the message and, one hopes, someone who speaks to you, live.

# 10

# TAKING TESTS

Tests are often part of the selection and promotion process in large organisations. Smaller ones too will usually administer proficiency tests in specific skills demanded by the job. Short tests may take place right after the interview. Even if you have qualifications, you may still be asked to take practical tests on your special skill, such as:

- Translating/Interpreting
- Desk editing
- Word processing/Typing
- Transcription from tape or shorthand
- Hairdressing.

Craft level entrants to the armed services and apprentices may be tested on their craft and technical knowledge generally.

## Pencil and paper tests

These timed tests are objective, so offer all candidates an equal chance of passing. However, practice beforehand can improve your score, and Kogan Page publish several books on how to pass them.

English language and numeracy are usually included in all tests, at various levels.

'English' may be tested under the guise of topics called variously: vocabulary, spelling, alphabetisation, correcting sentences with transposed words or phrases, arranging sets of sentences in a coherent order, verbal reasoning, verbal usage and reading comprehension.

Basic figure work could cover addition, subtraction, multiplication, division, numerical tasks involving them all, number sequences and numerical reasoning.

Multiple choice questions are often asked in timed tests. Each question comes with three or four possible answers; you choose the right one. Always put something down even if it is only a guess.

More specialist tests will check understanding and interpretation of information provided in the paper, for example:

- Business judgement: making decisions based on the information provided

- Data sufficiency: deciding whether the data provided will enable you to solve the set problem.

- Data interpretation

■ Logical reasoning: handling complex information and preparing reasoned arguments from it.

UK police forces set their test *before* the recruitment interview. In addition to sections from the above, a video-based observation test is set, as well as the transfer of data from one medium to another. The pass mark may be varied to relate the number of successful candidates to the current level of recruitment.

### Aptitude tests

These tests aim to reveal personality, motivation and abilities. They uncover an individual's potential, and will indicate to an employer the abilities that could be developed through training and experience on the job.

Verbal and numerical reasoning is included, as well as personality, interest and motivation question-naires.

A fuller explanation and practice material are to be found in *Test Your Own Aptitude* (Kogan Page).

## Assessment centres and group activities

These are both procedures for selecting and promoting at management level (also for officers in the armed forces). Candidates for jobs overseas may be required to undergo them too. They are expensive to run, often taking place at hotels or conference and activity centres, so are used mainly when the cost of changing personnel justifies them.

Written tests, interviews, practical exercises, group

activities and social events may form part of the programme.

Apart from being marked on the written tests, candidates are studied throughout the day or two's duration and assessed on their performance.

Components of the programme to warn you of include:

## Physical exertion, physical skills and outdoor exercises

These are especially used for the uniformed services, but business managers may be expected to go orienteering, climbing or go-karting, for example.

## Presentations

1. Autobiographical. You obviously concentrate on job-related achievements, motivation and aims, after a brief sketch of education and family. Try not to become emotional if you inadvertently touch a raw area.

2. A subject chosen by the candidate from a presented list. Preparation time will be short, or off the cuff. There may even be no choice of subject.

## Group discussions

1. A work-related problem to which the group is asked to suggest solutions. Candidates are marked on their participation, so make sure you contribute to all group work. Candidates are noted as being: natural leaders; bossy and overbearing; shy and

retiring; producing sound and sensible arguments; able to express themselves well; initiators; non-contributing.

2. General discussion of a political or social topic of the day, with or without a leader, which will reveal candidates' general knowledge, opinions, attitudes, ability to communicate ideas and present reasoned argument.

The employer may be looking for a leader or a good team member; your attitude and contribution are most important in this context.

### In-tray exercises

Candidates are presented with a heaped in-tray which they have to deal with in a set time.

## Social interaction

You will be eating together and socialising together. However relaxed the atmosphere becomes, never forget that you are being observed. How you handle alcohol will be noted; some people will elect to avoid it. Join in the activities enthusiastically, and enjoy yourself.

## Health and physique

It is as well to mention medical examinations here. A condition of the job offer may be a satisfactory health check. Depending on the job, there may be height and sight requirements. Make sure you pass before handing in your notice.

## 11

# WHEN CAN YOU START?

At last, the call you have been waiting for. Or did the offer come straight after your interview?

Either way, you need confirmation of the terms and conditions of your employment. If there is room for manoeuvre, this is the time to get the deal improved, or ask for time to think it over before giving your answer.

The offer may be conditional upon satisfactory references or a clean bill of health as evidenced by a medical examination by the company doctor. Ask about this.

## Your contract

Make sure you understand what the job entails before writing a letter of acceptance. Your contract o employment must be given to you within eight weeks of starting work and include:

- Job title and brief description of work
- Pay
- How you are paid
- Hours of work
- Paid leave (holidays)
- Length of notice on both sides
- Disciplinary and grievance procedures
- Pensions and pension schemes.

The contract is a legal document and should be looked after carefully.

Other points to check:

- Starting date (what notice must you give your present employer?)
- Whether existing holiday arrangements can stand
- When salaries are reviewed
- Whether there will be a special early review for new starters
- Whether employment is subject to completion of a satisfactory probationary period, and if there is a salary review at the end of it.

Many employers offer benefits as part of the remuneration package, depending on the level of job. They will probably have been mentioned during interviews, but should be confirmed in writing as part of the job offer. They range from free staff canteen to medical insurance, travel allowance, company car, bonuses, low-cost mortgage and help towards children's private education.

The employer's contract will cover more topics than the statutory version:

*Job title*
At the company's discretion you may be required at any time to transfer to another department or do other work which the company can reasonably request.

*Hours of work*
There may be no automatic extra payment for overtime.

*Payment during absence due to sickness or injury*
Payment over and above the legal requirement for Statutory Sick Pay may be at the company's discretion.

Give in your notice to your present employer only when the new job has been offered to you in writing and you have accepted – in writing – the offer made. You could otherwise fall between two stools and end up with no job at all.

All your hard work has paid off, and you have landed the job you wanted. You now have to make a success of it. Good luck!